Grandma
HAS
Alzheimer's
But It's OK

Grandma
HAS
Alzheimer's
But It's OK

MEMOIR

MARIAN TALLY SIMMONS BROWN

LitPrime Solutions
21250 Hawthorne Blvd
Suite 500, Torrance, CA 90503
www.litprime.com
Phone: 1-800-981-9893

Published by LitPrime Solutions   09/16/2022

ISBN: 979-8-88703-046-3(sc)
ISBN: 979-8-88703-047-0(e)

Library of Congress Control Number: 2022915939

Any people depicted in stock imagery provided by iStock are models, and such images are being used for illustrative purposes only.

Certain stock imagery © iStock.

Because of the dynamic nature of the Internet, any web addresses or links contained in this book may have changed since publication and may no longer be valid. The views expressed in this work are solely those of the author and do not necessarily reflect the views of the publisher, and the publisher hereby disclaims any responsibility for them.

Contents

Introduction

This story is about a special person – my grandma. Everyone knows what a grandma is because most families have them. Sometimes grandmas are inherited through friendships with schoolmates or acquaintances. Often times there are ladies at Church, the Synagogue, Kingdom Hall, in the neighborhood, or in civic and social clubs that parents attend who become grandmas to scores of children.

Another way we experience grandmas is through family stories passed down from generation to generation. When you see pictures of people in those stories, they become real to you.

Although they lived long ago and you've never met them, you begin feeling that you've known them all your life. Such is the power of the energy and spirit of grandmas to live on forever through their families.

Now family grandmas come in two's. You get one from your mom and one from your dad. Sometimes they live in your town, your neighborhood, down the street, next door, in your house, and sometimes far away. No matter the distance, for all the one-of-a-kind events in your life, grandmas seem to be there when needed, as when you were born. Grandma was there. If not right at the moment you came into the world, shortly thereafter. Her face was one of the first you saw after meeting mom and dad, and for the rest of your life grandma was there — smiling, cooing, coaxing, supporting, protecting, sharing, giving; always reminding us how special we were in her life.

This is the special gift grandmas bring to us – who, what, and why we are in our family, in the world. They spend their life helping us discover these things and because we are growing and changing all the time, they have to figure out different ways to get our attention so we'll remember the most important parts of ourselves. This makes them treasures, like all the special things we find and stash away in cubbies and secret places known only to ourselves. We can't hide grandmas away like butterfly wings, rocks, seashells, birds' nests, and empty Robin's eggs, but we can keep memories of time shared with them forever locked in our hearts.

There are two grandmas in my family and each one of them shared something special of themselves with me. Hearing of things they did as children in the rural South was like piecing together beautiful quilt squares that told the history of both sides of my family and revealed qualities that characterize me even down to personality traits. Now when I look at old family pictures, or meet cousins once or twice removed, I feel a strong kinship with them, not only through the physical features we share but also through the essence of spiritual strength passed down through legendary ancestors. Coming to know grandma in this story and sharing her life was to discover a treasure as exciting and as breathtaking as the beautiful rock I found while digging out in an open field near my mother's old family home place. It was one of the last treasures I remember stashing away before exiting childhood.

My Treasure

I remember the circumstances of the find "clear as day", as the grandma in this story would say. It happened as my cousin and I was out walking – ambling along, as was often the case in those days of growing up in the "country" as we called it then. At first, we were just walking aimlessly, kicking clumps of firmly formed clods of earth. Without any real reason, we stopped, stooped, and began turning up the soil with our bare hands, frequently taking time to smell the rich soil that filtered through our fingers. Soon our gentle nudging of the soil turned to more purposeful digging with sticks and bits of broken glass and whatever else we could find. Little by little, the rhythm of our unearthing accelerated as we seemed to be spurred on by memories of previous finds on our special expeditions in the woods and fields nearby. Soon the fast pace of our digging was matched by the crescendo of our taunting jibes to each other that we would not find anything special.

Suddenly, there it was, this visual splendor, glistening in the sunlight as if it had been waiting for me to uncover it. I did not know it was there particularly; yet, past experience had taught me the power and delight of the unexpected. As I reflect on the excitement of that moment, it must have been very much like that of this grandma as she awaited my birth. She did not know particularly whether I was a boy or a girl, only that she was getting her first grandchild. So, there she was with great expectation, heart and arms open wide to receive me as I made my entrance into the world and her family.

The love grandma had for her daughter, my mom, and all that she knew and experienced with a family whose physical features and characteristics I was an extension of, made me familiar to her even though I was just newly born. This was very much the situation with my treasure, my rock. Through previous pleasurable experiences on the spot where I found the rock, and because of the person who shared with me the moment of its discovery, my rock felt very familiar although I had never laid eyes on it before. Its familiarity lay in the shape of beans I had seen grandma cook in a black iron pot on her wood cook stove and in some of the parts I had seen inside chickens she prepared for Sunday dinner. As I stood in the open field alongside my cousin, looking at my rock, I was transported to a magical land of past associations. First of all, my rock was smooth like the marbles he had in his collection. It also reminded me of the new flooring grandpa put down in the house he built for one of my great uncles. He used a tool called a plane that was run across the wood to shave away knots and rough places of the long pieces of unfinished pine he got from the lumber yard. When he finished running the plane across the expanse of flooring, I could run all over it in my bare feet without getting splinters. What a special feel that smooth, hard, cool surface was.

My rock was not just a shape, it was also colors; not as many as you see in a kaleidoscope, but certainly more than one shade of what appeared to be green. Immediately, I was reminded of the color of rich, deep green, velvety moss that grew in the damp soil around my great uncle's house. There were many oaks there. Some of them were so large and old that their roots seemed to grow up from the earth, protruding above the ground like giant ribs of imaginary monsters. When I accompanied grandpa as he worked on my uncle's house I often played underneath the thick canopy of those oak limbs, placing wildflowers and fern on the moss-covered earth, creating a miniature sanctuary for crickets, beetles, and frogs I caught. So, you see, this was no ordinary rock, but a treasure as the grandma in this story became my treasure. She, like my rock, felt familiar to me although I was in an ongoing process of coming to know her, day by day as my life unfolded, becoming blended and interwoven with hers.

Her name and her whole being became one with all the pleasurable, enriching, fulfilling, and comforting things I experienced during times spent at her home. Events, tastes, and smells of those idyllic days are no less vivid in my mind than when they first occurred: the smell and taste of yeast dough on my finger after I ran it around the curve of a bowl while grandma was not looking; the smell of an old tattered hand-me-down quilt that covered me and grandma as we lay in one of the twin beds on which my mom was born; making mud pies in her backyard near where grandpa had his flower bed; tying a string to June bugs' legs and watching them soar like miniature effigy kites in the sultry Summer breeze; climbing my favorite dogwood tree, hanging upside down, pretending to be a cocoon; running in the yard at night with a jar of lightning bugs clasped in my hand; sneaking off with my cousin in search of forest springs as we looked for crayfish and salamanders; and splashing barefoot through muddy, warm rain puddles, getting "ground itch" between my toes. Just as these memories remain special, so is the grandma in this story. She, like all grandmas, seemed to have a particular genus all her own. No matter the time in which grandma lives, their style remains unequaled. They are able to elevate the simplest experience to an awesome adventure as I've heard my mom speak of the way her great grandma, Grandma Lawya, made bedtime the most exciting time of day just by heating an old "smoothing iron", (so-called because after being heated on top of the cook stove, literally, all it did was smooth wrinkles since it could get no hotter than you could comfortably hold its cloth-wrapped handle in your hand), wrapping it in a woolen cloth and placing it underneath the covers at the foot of the bed as a bed warmer in the dead of Winter.

Mom said she always looked forward to Grandma Lawya's visits because of the calm her spirit brought into the home. Grandma Lawya talked barely above a whisper and her entire physical presence reflected a special quietude. She was usually called upon during times of sickness because it seemed she knew just the remedy for all conditions, like the time she had grandpa go into the woods and bring back special leaves that they laid all over mom to break her fever and to make the rash "come out" all over her body when she had measles.

The leaves worked! Mom said she experienced Grandma Lawya's specialties one by one as a particular situation required them. Since she never knew what each visit would bring, having her in the home was like getting a bag of surprises tied with a string. Each day was uniquely different as mom anticipated a happening that would "pop" out of Grandma Lawya's imaginary sack. Although mom discovered Grandma Lawya's remedying skills sickness by sickness, the smoothing iron episode was repeated each night during Winter visits and throughout the day mom asked the question that reassured her of the magical moment that was to come, "Grandma Lawya, are you going to heat the iron tonight?"

The truth of the matter was Grandma Lawya was old and spoke of being chilled to the bone all the time. This was why she wore a long woolen petticoat underneath her dresses all year long and also accounted for her need for the smoothing iron in bed at night. The other reason was there was no central heating in the house mom grew up in. There was not even a fireplace in her bedroom. One entire side of the house was warmed in Winter by a gigantic wood-burning heater, so a bed warmer was necessary to reduce the crisp coolness of the 100% cotton starched and ironed sheets that grandma prided herself on using. Crawling into bed, situating herself underneath mounds of covers, feeling the warmth of that old cloth-wrapped smoothing iron was nothing short of a magical moment. In reality, only Grandma Lawya's feet touched the iron. Mom's legs were not long enough to reach it, but that didn't matter. Mom was there with Grandma Lawya, enfolded in her arms, their hearts melded into a single rhythm in a bed that could tell stories of the numerous relations for whom it had provided rest. The old woman's arms and her aged stories encircled mom like a cocoon, and as they shared their moment, night after night, mom became insulated in her imaginary casing by the strength and wisdom of the old woman, expressed in stories told of places she had farmed and people she had known. In looking back, mom realized the significance of those magical nights lay in the process of going through the motion of something so elemental, so simple, yet so profound. She had intently watched every step of the ritual: finding the iron, placing it on the red-hot heater, carefully removing it from the heater key so as not to get burned, wrapping it in woolen cloth to secure its warmth, and placing it just so at the foot of the bed. Somehow as she watched this age-old ritual, she made the connection between the old woman, herself, and all those who had done it before, surviving severe circumstances by figuring out how to use ordinary things to get extraordinary results. Great Grandma Lawya was mom's point of contact with them all. This was the magic. The clincher was, years later as mom returned to the source of her beginnings, she would discover the verity of her imaginings of being in a cocoon. Like the caterpillar she imagined so many years before as she hung upside down in her special tree in grandma's back yard, she too was metamorphosing, only it had taken a lifetime before she emerged from her casing more fully aware of who she was and what she could become – what she had become.

All grandmas have special things about them that highlight and dramatize who they are; things that indelibly imprint their image in your memory. Maybe it's the scent of their perfume, a special piece of jewelry, their pet name for you, or a piece of furniture that has always been in their house. It might even be plump feather pillows, a purse always filled with just what is needed for every imaginable situation, a lap that's the perfect width and depth for your size, or their inexhaustible supply of love. It is because of the grandma in this story that I came to discover all this but what makes her really special to me and our family is she has Alzheimer's. Yes, grandma has Alzheimer's but it's o.k. Going through the process with her taught my family more of the reality of life than we would have learned otherwise. Personally, I discovered it is under the most trying circumstances that the human spirit soars to untold heights. Perhaps the most poignant lesson of all was a realization that the sum total of life is a series of transitory situations very much like tasks, each requiring a particular level of understanding and skill to complete.

Rather than seeking ways to avoid possible discomfort these can bring, life should be lived one day at a time, moment by moment, applying the lessons of human experience to each encounter; for it is in this that we discover our greatest potential for love, compassion, understanding, and strength.

It was this approach to an all-encompassing, devastating condition that enabled my mom, grandma's only child, to not only rise to the occasion but remain at the helm, a veritable bulwark of strength and faith for all who knew her, leading our immediate family through the maze of unique experiences grandma's condition thrust upon us.

Yes, grandma has Alzheimer's and it would affect our entire family, even pets, but we would remain a family, and, from time to time, all under one roof. Fascinatingly, we would come to see that while grandma was medically losing control, she continued to positively impact those who were gathered around her. After more than thirty years, mom moved back to her childhood home to oversee the care of both parents; for while grandpa was on his feet and very capable, he would lose his sight to glaucoma. Grandpa, mom, Baby Sis, numerous nursing aides, and for a brief time, the Hallelujah Lady and Miss Sunshine, along with myself, assisted directly in the special care of grandma. All of us came to give something special of ourselves, but, in the final analysis, received, experienced, and learned more than any of us ever dreamed: that shared experience cements friendships; humility is indeed a virtue, and it is when we acknowledge our need for others that we really stand tall; that our lives do have their individual patterns; it is not for us to shirk our responsibilities; the divine creator really does have things under control, and, if we submit ourselves to Him, He will make our feet like hind's feet and we can ascend the rough places.

The Diagnosis

I knew something very big and very different was happening because mom made such frequent trips to grandma. When she returned, she seemed quiet, deep in thought; not particularly sad but very much preoccupied. Little-by-little whispers grew to open discussions and we finally acknowledged the diagnosis that sentenced grandma to a loss of self – Alzheimer's.

Traditional childhood diseases were the ones most familiar to me. Unlike these, Alzheimer's can be very insidious, smoldering for years before being declared. Mom said if a person had it family would see the signs, but if you don't know what you're looking for, as in a sequential pattern of behaviors, it is well on its way by the time the patient is medically diagnosed. In looking back, grandpa and mom agree, grandma was under the subtle siege of Alzheimer's for many years.

An obvious sign that something was happening within grandma was her loss of interest in doing things she had always been meticulous about; things that you do according to the hour of the day, such as going to bed at night, getting out of bed in the morning, taking a bath, brushing your teeth, combing your hair, putting on clothes, having a good time with friends and family, and keeping your general surroundings clean. This change did not take a clinical examination to determine. There were days of being dressed in only a nightgown and bedroom shoes with rollers in her hair. She did not exhibit the slightest bit of concern for her appearance, even when the doorbell rang announcing visitors. Her ever-present companion, grandpa, became an intimidator in her sight. This resulted in him spending long hours in the basement "piddling" around or down in the area where he had pet goats, while grandma was left to herself in the house with the phone as her link to the outside world. However, soon, it too became an interloper in her world, and old friends who called, with whom she had shared recipes, shopping, and just general run-of-the-mill life experiences, were shunned. These changes were of a greater impact on grandma directly than on her family, but her insomnia encompassed us all, completely disrupting the household, and wiping everyone out.

Grandma would sit up all night, not doing much of anything, plundering she called it, looking over old papers, going through dresser drawers, trying to find something, although she could not tell you what it was. If she found what she thought she was looking for or something she liked the looks of, she stacked it. Little by little her sleeplessness and plundering created little mountains of clothes and personal objects throughout the house. Sometimes grandpa's personal belongings became part of her mountains and retrieving them was impossible. As the situation intensified, grandpa began to realize that in very different ways he and grandma were losing parts of themselves to Alzheimer's. His solution was to try and retrieve what he could of grandma. He tried to coax her to bathe, comb her hair, to dress for the day. His efforts achieved visible results but under great duress. In the end, grandma's behavior became more agitated. In time we learned the stages of Alzheimer's were processes grandma had to go through. We could not reprogram her; rather, we had to deal with each symptom as it manifested itself. In other words, we had to stand back and give her the space she needed to go through her transformation. Day by day, grandma took center stage in her house and her family withdrew, taking with them the routines, the responsibilities, and the expectations that helped define the role she created and fulfilled in their lives. Grandma's role dysfunction was marked by memory loss. Interaction with people required multi-level skills that became increasingly more difficult for her to perform. We observed that as she forgot more and more of the things that took a lot of processing to remember, she could easily perform large motor skills, and these she repeated over and over again. For instance, grandma would get up in the morning and, as if programmed, prepare to iron. What broke our hearts was what she ironed – soiled laundry, anything she could find. Years ago, she had a routine of placing padding on one end of the island in the kitchen and "getting wrinkles out" of small items rather than putting up the ironing board. She remembered that routine, and day after day she ironed and while she ironed, she talked. Invariably it was the same story of her past, like a stuck needle on a record or a spot of dust on a CD, and we could only listen and watch. It was like a scene rehearsed for a play or maybe a playback of a movie you'd seen numerous times before. This playback was really complex because of the parts of herself grandma used in the picture. While her arms repeated the motion of ironing, her lips mouthed words, and her facial expression took on its own character. There was one scene but each part of the player seemed to be a separate entity unto itself. "What was happening to grandma?" our hearts silently screamed. Watching her made me feel like I did when learning to ride a bike or trying to swim. I had to get all the different parts to work together in order to move forward. One part of me had to control all my movements. It seemed that part of grandma that controlled everything was not functioning.

Yet, there was a part of her that remembered and it tried to hold on to make her family see that she was not all gone. That was the part that repeated itself. That was the part that continued to iron.

There were many signs of grandma's loss of self. Some were clearly visible while others were very subtle. Some that deeply unnerved onlookers were her silence, blank state, and apparent oblivion at attempts to draw her into conversation and family activity. Amazingly, of her own volition, though appearing to be in a trance, she could make verbal responses to comments and sometimes even ask thought-provoking questions.

The Many Faces
of Alzheimer's

O f all the signs we observed, the inability to process details and interrelated facts had the greatest overall impact on her total family relationships and home environment.

Grandma had always been the one to take care of money matters in her home. She could correctly figure columns of numbers in her head to the last penny. Every dime in her home was accounted for. Commercial sales of household goods, personal clothing, and groceries were methodically pursued and her stash of paper towels, toilet tissue, soap, washing powder, and dishwashing liquid, not to mention two stocked-to-the-brim freezers, were proof of her practical application of the axiom, "Prepare for need in the time of plenty."

Saving was always uppermost in her mind. She saved letters written by her grandmother some fifty years ago. She saved the locks of hair from her brothers' first haircuts. She saved pennies, everything. Alzheimer's made her forget the value of these treasures.

It also made her misplace cash, pay bills more than once, and sometimes not pay them at all. The other side of the coin was grandma stopped paying attention to money as something of value, period. She stashed it between pages of books and handed it out to those who were mere acquaintances. Mom said these were not just signs of grandma forgetting, it was grandma coming undone – unraveling like a ball of yarn. Right before our very eyes, we were seeing the parts that made grandma who and what she was as an individual and as an essential link in our family chain become dislocated. This made me think of R2D2 when he became short-circuited. Similarly, crucial circuits in grandma's control center were shutting down. However, those that remained functioning, were live wires.

Everyday routines and patterns of life at grandmas were changing and in some instances, being completely dissolved. Yet, grandpa felt there was still hope for keeping some semblance of the family life he had experienced with his wife of more than fifty years. To an extent this was true. Bills could be straightened out, money replaced, and grocery shopping is done. Grandpa did just that for as long as he could, but what no one could fix were grandma's mood swings.

Grandma's extensive sleepless nights were followed and sometimes accompanied by fits of rage and depression. There were harsh words and insults accorded friends whose phone calls were cut short in the curtest manner. Even mom's calls were quickly directed to grandpa. Day-by-day smiles turned to tightened facial muscles. It was as if grandma's features were being re-shaped. There was no doubt about it, as her moods grew more complex and outbursts more explosive, she took on a more stressful-looking appearance.

As I observed all these happenings with grandma, Alzheimer's began to remind me of the Parcheesi game I played as a child. In that game, you never knew what you would roll with the throw of the dice. Each day for our family was like the roll of dice in a game of chance.

Another way of looking at Alzheimer's is to see it as a kaleidoscope of behavior. Each day brought a shifting image of grandma. In moments she could move from childlike innocence, laughter, and expressions of love, to rage; from recoiling in fear at the threat of being touched to deafening silence, and an almost catatonic state. All the while, grandpa was there, shielding and protecting her from curiosity seekers and from the outside world. His pain in the matter was deep because Alzheimer's was a condition he could not fix. He did not have Alzheimer's. It had him and it placed him in the position of a ghost in a gothic novel. He was unable to make himself seen or heard by grandma. It was as if he was locked in a moment of time, trying to retrieve the past and the spirit of grandma he once knew. His inability to reach deep into her soul and jar her sensibilities made him feel more the prisoner of Alzheimer's than she.

There were other signs that measured the extent of grandma's drifting into the isolation of Alzheimer's. One was the appearance of her closet. First of all, it was a small closet because houses built over forty years ago on modest incomes were more functional than luxurious. Rather than walk-in closets, wardrobes and armoires were the norms. Anyway, back to grandma's closet. Immediately upon opening the door, you knew the message being sent from the central command of the person who organized it was being intercepted.

Instead of being aligned in the same direction on the clothes bar, hangers were sticking in every direction. There were hangers on the bar and hangers-on hangers. Hangers were right side up and upside down. The entire scene made me think of a wire monster or lots of insects' legs all jumbled up. If this was an outward sign of how she perceived her surroundings, grandma must have felt like people say you do when you wake up from a deep sleep, disoriented and unaware of the time, the day, and even who or where you are. I've heard mom describe the sensation as "feeling disconnected" and panic-stricken. That's the way grandma's closet looked as if there was no connection made between what the hangers were and how they were to be used.

Another sign of great change in grandma was the expression on her face. I always had a lot of fun with grandma because she could make a great joke out of anything; laughing until she lost her breath. Now the range of possibilities for her facial expression seemed sorely limited.

Her jawline had become set into a hard position. This created the image of her teeth being locked together as in the instance of a person who has just tasted a green sour apple or a very sour pickle. When she wasn't in a more relaxed mode her lips were often tightly drawn together and her breathing flowed through nostrils flared at the ends, giving the appearance of grandma being in a constant rage. Sometimes her eyes took on a wild, wide-eyed look. The softness once there when grandma and I had our fun-filled moments was all gone. These were physical signs but there were other signs as well. One seemed innocent enough but it could make grownups blush with embarrassment, especially if they were strangers. It was grandma's childlike expression of love. She told the medical doctor she loved him, and the pharmacist at the drug store we frequented, the cashier in the grocery store, everybody. Of course, the people she addressed were unnerved, responding only with a bewildered look. Grandpa would just take her by the arm, smile, nod his head, and move along.

During this stage of her condition, grandma's speech was still clearly audible. She was very capable of analyzing any situation as she perceived it and demanded that she be paid honor, although her verbiage was repetitive, and at times, out of control. One demand clearly understood and often expressed was "Take me to the Mall"! No matter how hard they tried, she could not be calmed down or dissuaded from going shopping. The intensity of her demand was matched by her obsession to purchase lingerie of every variety, especially slips and girdles. This was at least three years before mom moved back home. During this time grandma and grandpa took the train to visit her and grandma's suitcase was filled with the fruits of her labor in the Mall – panties, slips, girdles, and bras. She had not packed one stitch of outer clothing.

Another obvious sign of grandma's condition was what mom called her "willfulness". Whatever popped into grandma's mind was what she was going to try to do. Grandpa related to mom and how he and grandma were all dressed for church one Sunday morning when she got it into her head that she had to sweep the curb in front of their house. On this particular Sunday, they were riding to church with a neighbor, and although the ride was there, grandma got the broom and swept, and all everyone could do was sit, watch, and wait for her to finish.

Often times grandma's willfulness got in the way of quality family time, like all the times she just plain refused to go to dinner at what was once her favorite restaurant. She'd get that tight-jawed, lips-pursed together, nostril-flared, breathing- hard look and we'd all just sit down, defeated, whipped without ever a lick being passed.

Imagine, all these varied and very complex shifts were occurring in grandma and for a while commitment to the family unit she helped knit together, of which she had been a part for over fifty years, compelled her to take up the slack, so to speak, especially in the early days of grandpa's waning vision.

Immediately preceding grandma's diagnosis of being in the intermediate stages of Alzheimer's, she drove. Just as grandpa would take over the cooking, handling the household finances, doing laundry, and paying bills when grandma could no longer maintain her role in the family, she took over driving when his sight began to dim. She drove to the grocery store, to church, and to the shopping center. She even drove through three states to visit mom. Their last interstate driving excursion cost thousands of dollars because when the red engine light came on signaling difficulty underneath the hood, grandma just kept on driving. Not for once did she glance at the dashboard to check for anything. A seven-day planned trip became a fourteen-day vacation, costing thousands of dollars, which was all the visible proof mom needed to remove any doubts about the growing severity of changes taking place in her parent's lives.

Mom lived three states away and although she came home twice a month to check on things, she was not able to evaluate the situation on a day-to-day basis. Her dear life-long friend kept her abreast of things and when she called to tell mom about a hair-raising incident following the interstate situation, mom had a plumb natural born fit. Even now, recalling the event brings chills to my spine. That incident was among a few others that flashed warnings as unmistakable as a Broadway Marquee that something would have to be done soon. Each of the incidents relayed to mom seemed to demonstrate a level of sense disorientation within grandma. One of the most harrowing occurred during the Fall season. Grandpa had an eye appointment and no one can understand why he did not take a cab, knowing his eyes would be dilated, placing grandma in the position of chauffeur without him as a guide. From what grandpa said, by the time the appointment was over it was dusk and rain had begun to fall. He could not see well enough to give grandma directions; consequently, she lost her bearings. I concluded she must have felt disconnected like the arrangement of hangers in her closet and like awakening from a deep sleep with no recollection of who or where she was. Although grandpa could not see clearly, intuitively he felt they were lost. He had no idea where they were and grandma could not identify any familiar landmarks to give him a clue as to where they might be. So, grandma drove, the rain poured, and it grew darker. By the grace of God, grandma ended up on the major thoroughfare near their neighborhood and was finally able to give grandpa a familiar landmark that enabled him to direct her home. Grandpa relayed to mom that after everything was over, grandma never spoke a word about that incident one way or the other.

In assessing the situation, mom felt grandma got overstimulated by the compounding sound of the rain on the roof with the brightness of the headlights from on-coming traffic. There was no doubt about it, something had to be done at grandpa's and grandma's, and "with the quickness".

Soon after this, following endless discussions and pursuing numerous avenues for information about care options, our family opened its doors to in-home assistance because grandma reached the point of being incapable of taking care of her personal hygiene. Whereas we viewed this as necessary, grandma saw it as an intrusion into her domain: a strange woman in her kitchen, in her bedroom, bathing her. "Why, I never heard of such a thing", she hollered. She lashed out with all kinds of verbal abuse and demeaning epithets and when she could, she became physical, the results of which remain on her body to this day.

During one of her bouts of overt physical response, the situation took on the looks of an animated cartoon. On that particular day, a social worker came by at grandpa's behest to evaluate the situation. Grandma flew into a rage bereft with colorful vernacular and ran from the main part of the house down into the basement. There was grandma followed by grandpa, who, in turn, was followed by the social worker. From the basement, they retraced their steps up the stairs into the main house, then out the front door, into the street.

It was at the front door that a tussle between grandma and grandpa occurred, both pulling in opposite directions. As grandma struggled to get away, her upper back area was thrust against the corner of the open door, and from the pulling and twisting, she sustained a bruise that lasted for months.

At this stage of her condition, we never saw such physical strength, nor had we seen such intense rage. Where was all this coming from inside grandma? As she kept up her resistance, one aide had her glasses broken and all of them endured great hostility at their efforts to provide daily personal care. Grandma was still very much on her feet and it just seemed so invasive to have strangers undressing her and bathing her private parts, and she continued to make her feelings about this known in no uncertain terms. However, in time, her resistance lessened and everyone breathed a sigh of relief because the care being provided was so greatly needed.

Grandma was not the only one who had needs in this situation.

Grandpa and mom were suffering deeply. There was the pain of observing all these changes without a prescription for how to make it better. The solution was to respond to the symptoms. In this regard, the family would have to permanently lose a level of privacy as we opened our home to a series of strangers, better known as C.N.A.'s (certified nursing assistants). They came and they went. We never had one individual for more than twelve months. To supplement their presence, we hired sitters who did just that – they sat and watched grandma. They watched her sit and stare, watched her lie on the sofa and stare, and watched her walk a familiar path throughout the house until she grew tired, finally succumbing to sleep.

During this time perhaps the greatest challenge for the family was coming to understand that whatever difficulties the workers had in completing their assignment was not in their inefficiency, but in the ravages of Alzheimer's on the total being of grandma. All of us were accused by grandma of betraying her trust. We saw our loved one regress to a state of only being capable of base behavior. Although we knew we were unable to do anything about it, grandma's attitude made us feel as if we were the culprits. As dark as the hour of our realization of the depth and breadth of grandma's transformation, there were vestiges from her past, as we had known her, that showed 'round about us in that bleak time.

Ironing was one of the behaviors that spoke profoundly of grandma's previous way of life. Mom often spoke of how grandma's windows were dressed in white stiffly starched organdy curtains. Not only did she iron her curtains, but towels, sheets, pillowcases, clothing, and grandpa's under shorts as well. She kept the house the old-fashioned way. There was a wash day and an uninterrupted ironing day. Both were major events, nothing short of rituals, involving required materials, preparation time, as well as their own unique accompanying conversation. So, when grandma went through the motion of ironing, she was attempting to recreate a dynamic dimension of herself that her mind had not yet completely relinquished. Her life revolved around caring for her family, physical work when she was younger, going to church, participating in church-related activities, such as The Floral Club, Women's Missionary Circle, and, of course, Sunday School, and sharing with others. These activities defined her and it was through her attempts to continue functioning in them, where she could, that her spirit spoke to us in the strongest manner.

My grandma was a beautiful woman. She loved to dress for special occasions and going to church on Sunday was one of those.

Grandma was a hat lady. She had hats made completely of feathers, of fur; hats made of straw and lace; of netting, fruits, flowers, and bows, and each hat had its own companion outfit. There were shoes of leather, snakeskin, and patent, with bags to match. The finishing touch for grandma were gloves. There were wrist length and three-quarter length;

white, and all the colors of the rainbow. There were gloves of cotton, serge, and leather. Boy, could she put an outfit together. Following her ironing obsession, grandma entered her "dressing up every day" phase, and always she declared her destination to be at the church.

Just as she meticulously prepared her stage for ironing, she got out of bed and began her ritual of assembling and putting on her fancy "Sunday-go-to-meeting" clothes. She did this even before the aide came to help her with her personal care and it was "hell to pay" if anyone dared try to undress her. After dressing, regardless of the temperature, she would top off her outfit with a mink stole. Then she would go into the living room, lie down on the sofa and stay there the remainder of the day – not talking – just lying there, staring up at the ceiling.

One day grandma took getting ready for church to the limit. It was on a Saturday in the Summer and Mom had already moved back home. Grandma had completed her ritual of getting dressed and we thought she was in the den. Now, one characteristic grandma often exemplified was a kind of deviousness. It came across as "sneaky" behavior. As carefully as mom watched her, grandma slipped out of the den, through the kitchen, past mom, through the dining room, down the hall, and, as difficult as the lock was to manipulate, unlocked the front door and walked out of the neighborhood.

Mom said intuition led her to the front door. Of course, she found it standing wide open. Grandma was gone. When the verbal outcry was given, grandpa bounded up the stairs from the basement where he had been in solitude, and he and mom ran into the street. A chain reaction was set into motion. Mom got into her car, I got into mine, our cousin into his, and along with a neighbor, four cars went all around the neighborhood and onto the adjacent thoroughfare, but no grandma.

Mom and I continued our search. Still no grandma. After a while, all of us returned home to find several neighbors congregated in front of our house. We resembled a flock of geese that had lost its leader. There we were literally turning around and around in the middle of the street, without a clue as to what to do or where to go.

After grandpa had gotten his wits about him, he called a church deacon and the assumption was a search party would be formed but up to this point, no one had arrived. Minutes seemed to turn to hours as we talked amongst ourselves and sought comfort in each other's presence and prayers.

As we considered our next step, we noticed a van moving slowly down the street. As it came to a stop, who should step out but grandma, all dressed up, looking like a month of Sundays, without the slightest bit of concern at our presence in the street or our verbal outcries. As the driver of the van talked of his encounter with grandma, he relayed what we well knew. When she dressed up her talk was about going to church. From what the gentleman told us we were able to surmise what had happened. After exiting the house, grandma moved quickly to the main traffic corridor, even with high heel shoes and an arthritic ankle. An attentive individual could have quickly detected that she was disoriented. An aged woman walking through the neighborhood, completely dressed in a hat and mink stole in Summer was certainly not the norm. Mercifully, God permitted grandma to be found by a special couple. When the gentleman coaxed her into his van, she could only give key words, "church" and the name of her street. The couple took time to begin driving at one end of our street, which is intersected by a busy connector, continuing to the other end, believing someone would be standing outside, as we were, looking for a lost family member. That incident shocked our senses and made us necessarily aware of what Alzheimer's patients are capable of. We could not underestimate grandma, and definitely would have to "grandma-proof" the house. As long as she was on her feet, we would have to keep up efforts to outwit her attempts to "fly the coop".

While grandma's Alzheimer's was causing a loss of self, it was also revealing to us just how many parts we have to lose. There were parts she had never shown as long as she was in control, but once she began to be "disconnected" those hidden parts came out. We know the parts of ourselves we choose to reveal and the parts we choose not to reveal to others. I guess it's like the layers of clothing we wear. Everybody knows most people wear underclothes. Although we can't see the specific kind they are, we know they're there.

Our outer clothing helps us blend in with everybody else and people size us up, so to speak, by what they see on the outside. It's when we begin showing the secret parts – those more private parts – our under clothing that defines us in a more personal way, revealing the real us, without affectation, that people get nervous. Grandma began showing that part of herself that grownups know we have yet to keep private. This was the darker side of her condition, but the world is filled with contrasts and the sun rose on that dark side and we learned to find humor in grandma's multiple behaviors which at times seemed choreographed to get grandpa's goat.

One way grandma accomplished this was by playing games of hide and seek. When grandpa tried to locate her in the house, she ran and hid behind draperies in the living or dining room. The only clue to her whereabouts were the tips of her shoes that stuck out from underneath the drapery hems. She'd hide in the shower stall behind the shower curtain, and sometimes in her closet. When we'd find her, we would laugh, not sacrilegiously, but cathartic belly laughs that made our spirits rekindle the lightheartedness of youth grandma's antics put us in touch with.

When grandma was diagnosed in the intermediate stages of

Alzheimer's she was three score years and ten. It takes mastery of a great many higher-order thinking skills to efficiently function within your environment and interact with others in a socially acceptable manner for that period of time. In observing grandma from day to day, it became necessary for me to reconcile her coming undone, so to speak, with the role she fulfilled in our family and my personal emotional need to accept her transformation, to let her go; all the while, remembering that regardless of her physical changes, the essence of her spirit would remain with us through our memories.

I searched for a familiar reference point from which to try to analyze her behaviors. I found it in an unusual place, a connect-the-dots page of the newspaper. The association I made with grandma was that she could not always connect the right sequence of dots to get a clear picture of what an object was, how she should use it, why she needed to use it, and the consequences of its misuse. Her command center was not properly computing the impulses it received. She looked at the commode but used a trash can instead. She would perform a bodily function anywhere. Behavior that would have been unacceptable to her before the onset of Alzheimer's was now the norm. So, when we grandma-proofed the house we placed receptacles in all the places we thought she might look for one – behind curtains and doors; underneath beds, tables; in corners – everywhere. Grandma kept us on the move and as we attempted to outwit her, we found release for our intensity of purpose in laughter, at the memory of times past, and in the pain of the present. In both instances, we laughed to stave off tears.

A distinguishing part of grandma's personality that she lost was compassion for her pets. For as long as I remember, pets were members of our family. Pets had a particular and special place in our home and everyone knew that. The backyard speaks to the reverence grandma and grandpa held for pets in the number of its graves for cats, dogs, birds, and turtles. The last dog grandma raised came as a foundling. Though saved from certain death, he still suffered from being taken from his mother before being weaned. He became grandma's baby. She bottle-fed and burped him as if he were human.

Though he reached a height and weight excessive for puppy antics, he continued to physically show love for grandma and find comfort in her presence by placing his head on her shoulder or in her lap and his paws literally around each side of her neck. However, as grandma lost her ability to connect, her beloved pet suffered from her disorientation as other family members did. His presence agitated and frightened her and he, like all of us, could only stand frozen in the place of expectation, looking out at what was happening. None of us were able to take ourselves out of that place or bring grandma into it. She was pushing so much of herself aside. There were pieces of her lying all around, but, as Humpty dumpty, there was nothing that could be done by anyone of us to reassemble her.

By this time the severity of grandma's changes was underscored by the pressing need for mom to make a decision about returning home. Grandpa's face revealed in graphic manner the pain and frustration of trying to cope with a situation for which there was no tried and true formula that guaranteed positive results. For some time, he had dealt with grandma's condition as if it were a secret to be kept from everyone – even mom. Then he began pursuing a medical diagnosis, but after scores of tests, grandma was only more agitated; for she interpreted all the procedures as an invasion of her privacy as well as an indictment of her ability to maintain her role and position in the family.

Though perceived as a villain, grandpa continued to seek a solution relying on his own abilities. He tried giving grandma space to do what she determined had to be done. He sat quietly through her tirades, accusations, and hurling of epithets. He tried reasoning with her.

He prayed. No matter what he tried, grandma's intensity remained constant. There was no letup. He lived in fear of "what ifs". He could not see his way.

Grandma's change brought pain to us because we were helpless in making our discomfort go away. She did not know all we did about what was happening to her. This made the situation very much like that of a Greek tragedy. The audience is completely aware of all the circumstances and precipitating factors surrounding the hero and his situation. He, on the other hand, is without a clue. That was grandma. In spite of all the pain and severity of the losses all around her, grandma was unable to verbalize how she was at the center of it all. I also saw her as someone in the ocean being swept out to sea. Grandpa was in the ocean with her but compared to him, she was drifting smoothly. He was fighting against the flow. His was a struggle that only made him gulp down more water. Like a drowning man, he was flailing his arms, kicking his feet, slowly going under. Someone had to throw him a life jacket quickly. Mom was moving closer to her decision.

Many years earlier, I often heard Mom talk with her spiritual sister about life patterns. One of the more poignant statements I remember her making was she believed everyone is prepared all their life for that one great performance – that one thing more demanding than anything you've ever done, that one thing that requires more of the best of what we are or ever could be. At the time of that analogy, though she may not have known it, she was laying the psychological groundwork for her later life-changing decision to move back to her childhood home and oversee grandma's and grandpa's care for the remainder of their natural days.

A Mid-Life,
Life-Changing Decision

om's decision was no small matter. Before she could begin the first step she had to work on her head, so to speak. Furthermore, she needed to make certain she was not being motivated merely by her emotional response to the situation. All available literature at that time emphasized family hardships of patient care. Alzheimer's is a totally neurologically decimating condition. There would be no part of grandma untouched by its destructive force. How well could mom bear up under such force?

In recollecting steps in her decision-making, mom believes the most important thing she did was to begin acting on her belief that a higher power is in control, has a plan for each of us, and in order to discover what that is, we must submit. This enabled her to place the total situation within the cosmic sphere. In other words, her decision and its total ramifications on her life had to extend beyond the immediacy of grandma's needs. This thought process was absolutely essential for mom to be able to continue on beyond grandma's demise, should she live to see it.

As for the family's hardship, mom saw life as a process of accepting challenges and turning them into positive life builders. How would we ever know what we could become without challenges? Furthermore, she believed she began to be prepared for this special performance from the moment she was drawn up to the front of her church at eight years of age by what she felt was a "magnetic" force, testifying that she believed in Jesus – in front of hundreds of people, without so much as a prior warning to her parents. She just marched right up there and bravely answered the preacher's question about her profession of faith. This was the first step of her "submission" and it would remain a lifelong process. Mom said she vividly remembers the drop-jawed look on grandpa's face when she stood up. He didn't try to stop her. She couldn't stop herself. The power of that magnetic pull was too strong.

It was her belief in the power of submission, and her willingness to step out and begin her life pattern, that got her through difficult days. In fact, no one would believe her life if they didn't know it was true. As a child, getting up at five in the morning, walking through the family cemetery with her dad to catch a ride into town where she'd go to Granny Rena's house and go back to bed because it was so early, then arise a second time and catch public transportation to the vicinity of the school, to walk the remainder of the way from the bus stop. Her difficulty getting to school was not a one-time thing but lasted the entire eight years she lived twelve miles outside the city limits, hence outside her school district, on the forty acres of land purchased by grandpa in the 1940s. Through it all she did not complain. Her parents accepted the struggle of transporting her into town because they believed it was their responsibility to provide her with the best educational opportunity they could.

Although a child, she was able to perceive the essence of their strength to deal with difficult odds and not be defeated by them. This groomed her ability to face future difficulties and demonstrated to her the quality of her lineage.

Mom did go home again, and, yes, there were times she couldn't see her way; yet, deep within herself, she believed everything would work out. After all, when she was driving up to see her parents twice a month, from her home three states away, she closed each visit with "I'll be here when you need me", and she meant every word. However, when she spoke those words, she did not see their full reality. In the natural, it looked so complex and it was because there was so much involved in physically moving from point A to point B. Little did she know her decision would grant her some of the most rewarding times of her mature life. As for her personal growth, she would come face to face with attitudes, emotions, beliefs, and memories that shaped her from infancy to adulthood.

Enriched life experiences and disciplined behavior accrued for over four decades would help mom understand grandpa, grandma, and herself to a greater extent than she ever would have without returning home. As this process began, mom saw it as validation of the purpose of her decision. It was for more than the immediacy of grandma's condition. It was also about mom's fulfillment of her life pattern. Then there were the people she'd meet – jewels she called them, placed in her path by the good Lord who always provides gifts whose warranties do not run out.

Yes, mom returned home but not without great pain. She left after high school to attend college, following that there was graduate school, a family, and a career, and over forty years later, she was returning as a mature adult; yet, to her parents she was ever the child. When mom returned this was the situation: grandma was in the intermediate stage of Alzheimer's and was losing parts of herself. Grandpa still had himself but because he and grandma were part of a single unit, he felt lost and saw no future for himself when grandma lost him completely. The family dog was out of the house because he made grandma feel frightened and agitated. Mom's thirteen-year-old Siamese developed a neurosis because her life had been so drastically disrupted by the move and mom's complete absorption by her parents' condition and the requirements of settling in. Her refusal to take solids or liquids led to dehydration and she had to be hospitalized. If this were not enough, grandpa's ego responded to mom's presence as a threat to his position as head of the house. No matter, mom unpacked, began organizing everything, beat the bushes, found a job, and began discovering the realities of caregiver for aged parents. What a thief Alzheimer's is.

Alzheimer's is a thief because it robs a person of the ability to know themselves, and their surroundings, and also by attacking the parts that keep us together as a family unit. It also robs the physical home because it disrupts established patterns. This can be a positive thing, but in the beginning grandpa, especially, saw it as an invasion of privacy and a dislocation of personal turf. He could not have been more correct. When mom returned home, nothing was left unexamined – important papers, clothing, family valuables, the kitchen pantry – every jot and tittle. This facilitated maintenance of grandpa's dignity as his sight grew dim because things he used daily were placed so that he could put his hands on them. This also facilitated the job performance of our in-home help, but lurking in our minds was "were they trustworthy?" Mom could tell by looking in her pantry if the food had been prepared for her parents; however, looking in the pantry would not tell her if time was given to make certain grandma ate sufficiently.

There was no question, we needed all the pairs of hands we could get. As we worked our way to the level of assurance of quality care we have now, we tried ladies who just sat and watched grandma, and while they were a necessary and important part of grandma-proofing the house, they were not classified as professional, from the standpoint of how they assessed and responded to grandma's changing behaviors. We knew what was happening in our home was discussed with others. Momentarily it made us feel uncomfortable but that lasted for about one second. There was only time for moving forward positively.

It was agreed without saying, our approach to grandma would be as if she were a child in the position of learning a skill that required coordination of many parts. The situation was made complex because there was no one grandma could communicate with to express how she felt or what she thought would help pull all her parts together. Her medical diagnosis had been given to our family, but mom was working in the trenches, learning as she plowed through everything, and the furrows she was working were deep.

By the time mom returned home, Grandpa's sight had dimmed considerably; yet, his hospital orderly training and his work experience provided invaluable skills needed in the care of grandma, but we still needed additional pairs of hands. More specialized assistance came in the form of certified nursing assistants who prepared food, bathed, fed, and dressed grandma. These dear ladies suffered through grandma's verbal and sometimes physical abuse. In a phrase, they tried to help grandma keep herself together. At this stage, it was very much like looking after a toddler because grandma was still on the move throughout the house. Gradually, she wound down to the point of lying on her favorite sofa for long periods of time, and everyone took a deep breath.

It took some doing, but mom finally got everything organized so that the house could run on a schedule without her constant physical presence. Everything was put into a special place and there it has remained until this very day. This proved especially helpful for grandpa.

Now he was assured he could always put his hands on what he was looking for as he memorized its location. Imagine that – food in the kitchen cabinets, in the refrigerator, personal care and cleaning items in the bathroom, in his chest of drawers, the closet, the basement – everything had its very own spot. To say mom was busy was an understatement. It seemed she never slowed down.

On weekends in particular she strove to keep grandma's senses stimulated so she would not lose so many parts of herself at once. So, she loaded both parents up on Saturdays, and away they went: out into the country to the old family home place to visit cousins; for drives to neighboring towns for ice cream; in town and out-of-town to restaurants; she even took them to an outdoor concert in the park.

She took them with her when she got manicures, parking close to the facility so she could watch them, making certain grandma did not try to exit the car. On Sundays, she packed them up for church, and, of course, they visited special friends. At Christmastime she drove them through the city to see the lights; they walked through the Mall, grandma in her wheelchair and grandpa holding onto mom's arm. Grandma enjoyed these outings. She smiled, pointed, and waved at everyone who passed by. Jokingly, grandpa responded that they were probably thinking only a crazy person would take on two liabilities such as mom had. They did not know my mom. She took on commitments 100%. She vowed to see this to the end. She not only said it, she believed that the good Lord would see her through this and she did not hesitate to let out a "Hallelujah" in praise every now and then as a testimony to her faith in God to sustain her through it all.

For the first two years, after mom returned home, everybody attended church. Sometimes grandma talked out loud, but most of all, she enjoyed being made to look pretty. However, little by little the crowds began making her feel uneasy. Most times after church, mom took grandma and grandpa to their favorite restaurant and it was there that our family made very special friends.

In most eateries there are regulars. In our restaurant, some of these regulars began to make special efforts to exchange pleasantries which grew into hugs, pats on the shoulder, and words of encouragement to mom. This really made mom feel good. It would have been difficult not to see that she was with two elderly people with special needs. Even the owner regularly stopped to chat and sometimes help them get situated at their table. One day she even gave mom a beautiful lily to wear as a corsage. At other times strangers would come up to offer assistance, especially after grandma began using a wheelchair. Friendships made at that restaurant have continued and include the owner, waitresses, hostesses, and cashiers. The owner and members of her staff are part of what mom calls her affirming contingency, in other words, special people God placed in her path at special times for very special situations.

Coping Strategies

Mom continued to maintain her stimulation process throughout the home. Grandpa had one parakeet, mom got the second one, along with a canary with an audio tape to encourage it to sing, and, happily, Chang, mom's aging Siamese cat began to adjust to her new surroundings. Everyone, even the animals had something special that they brought to the vibrancy of the setting mom was creating. The birds lent their voices. Chang's antics brought laughter; especially her routine of moving from room to room, following the sun's rays as she sought warmth for her arthritic joints. However, the big boost we got in the pet department came in the form of a stray Siamese-mix, who was literally "dumped" in our yard, whom I named Pharaoh.

He was just what the house needed. From a young kitten, he attached himself to grandma, going into the bathroom with the aides, sitting on the side of the tub, and watching grandma get her bath. He loved the water, grandma feared it, but his presence provided just the distraction grandma needed so the aide could do her job. Pharaoh became grandma's companion as she walked through the house. What a funny, heartwarming sight it was to see him weaving in and out of her legs, his long tail curling around like smoke from an outdoor campfire. Sometimes as grandma sat in her recliner he jumped in her lap and sniffed her face. Later as she became more prone to staying in bed all day, it was not uncommon to find him walking the four corners of her hospital bed. And when she let out verbal responses to having her position shifted or to being changed, he'd make his way underneath the bed where he sprawled, overseeing what all the commotion was about.

Speaking of bed, grandma and grandpa continued sharing their bed for at least four years after mom returned home, despite all the physical changes taking place with grandma. Grandpa felt it would be a shock to make a drastic change in the bedroom that had been theirs for over four decades. So, the familiar four-poster bed, with its fish net canopy, and Martha Washington bedspread remained in place until grandma's physical movements became routinely uncontrollable.

Gradually, and as if on schedule, grandma's systems showed to a greater degree the ravages of her medical diagnosis. Steps were made more slowly and arm movements from plate to mouth were less certain. Grandma continued to talk but her command center did not always compute appropriate responses. Gradually, her speech became more erratic and sounds became less clear. Neurological changes in grandma affected her ability to focus her eyes. Overall, there was a definite change in the look at her physical self and her ability to respond to external stimuli.

Grandma's growing loss of control indicated it was time for a wheelchair. Although this measured the extent of her progression into Alzheimer's, it enabled us to get her around easily and safely. The only problem we encountered was the time she decided to get out of the chair, falling to the floor, requiring Emergency Medical Personnel to help her up. From that time on we used restraint to secure her, easing our fears that she would hurt herself, as she continued to try to reclaim herself by returning to faintly remembered routines. A concern relative to the wheelchair was how to keep grandma from beating her lower legs against the footrests. Having difficulty bending her knees and keeping her feet on the rests, she preferred to stretch her legs out and rhythmically bounce them against the rests. Although removing the rests lowered the risk of sustaining bruises to her legs, it did not stop her from continuing to bounce them, hence, her heels against the floor, creating a continuous patterned thumping sound throughout her waking hours.

Life is a series of trade-offs. We become very efficient at balancing them as we move along our passages. Placing grandma in a wheelchair ensured ease of mobility but sitting for long periods of time resulted in her becoming constipated. The other option of spending long hours in bed impeded the flow of blood to her tissues. The happy medium was to make sure grandma consumed adequate fluids and vegetables and received rotation and motion exercises. Mom's responsibility was to stay on top of everything that affected grandma's total being. She checked and double-checked, reported to the physician, and said, "It is good."

As grandma continued to progress through the stages of Alzheimer's, she soon needed adult diapers. The four-poster bed was disassembled and the hospital bed went up. This was an emotional and psychological milestone for all of us because we were moving away from a way of life that never would be resurrected. The warm and comforting side of this change was that grandpa wished to remain in the bedroom with grandma, so we put up one of a pair of twin beds that he and grandma had gotten during the early years of their marriage. Great sentimentality surrounded those beds because mom was born in one of them and they later became part of her childhood bedroom furniture. Those beds had been slept in by many of our relatives and friends. Mom had shared them with playmates and school friends. Both of her grandmothers and great-Grandma Lawya had slept there. The beds were a mnemonic device for recounting family history and now one of them had been called forth to continue the legacy of preservation for a future time.

While the hospital bed marked an outward major physical change in grandma, it was matched by internal changes that we were unable to effectively ascertain. There was one very obvious change, however, and it was our difficulty to get grandma to ingest solids and liquids by mouth. There was no doubt about the outstanding quality of grandma's in-home care; yet, for a brief time she suffered dehydration. From that mom learned the best of care can be provided, but if a person is not closely monitored, they can suffer a form of starvation right before their very eyes. Grandpa sometimes called mom "Eager Beaver," because she was always going over everything with the aides; yet, that did not prevent this medical concern. The time had arrived for the G tube. Early in mom's return, she had seen an old acquaintance who cautioned her to work closely with her family physician who would advise her on what to do sequentially. However, mom discovered you cannot always rely on outside assessment. You have to be observant, ask intelligent questions, as well as make suggestions as a family member. The G tube was a solution for monitoring food and liquid intake. Grandma's color, skin texture, and overall condition improved immediately!

Grandma continued to progress in her condition and mom was growing in her potential. When the above- mentioned acquaintance remarked about the number of years she had kept her husband at home on a G tube, mom's then lack of experience caused her fear and trembling, but she was finding the truth of Philippians 4:13, "I can do all things through Christ which strengtheneth me". She realized this as she determined to take on this commitment to not let things get her down. She translated her parents' reality as having been entrusted with a stewardship. Grandma and grandpa were her jewels and she had to find ways to enable them to continue giving off lustre. She could not do that by moping around. One conversation she refused to be drawn into was the one that began "Girl, I don't see how you do it". She wasn't doing it. Its success was not because of her natural strength. It was her reliance on God to activate within her and all around her the necessary forces to make it happen. This was not a glorifying mom time but a testimony to the power and mercy of God's time. In her home, drooping shoulders and a hung down head- in- your- hands posture were not permitted. She often walked behind grandpa like a command sergeant, telling him "Perk up. Step up your pace. Hold your head up".

While mom was doing everything, she could to keep grandpa "up", who was motivating her? I Corinthians 1:27 tells us "But God hath chosen the foolish things of the world to confound the wise". Well, no doubt about it, mom's actions had confounded folk. Grandpa frequently told her she took on a job few would volunteer for. She made a lifestyle change, taking a job at thousands of dollars less than what she had been making, leaving a substantial career and all its potential at a time in her life when it seemed imprudent to do so.

However, six years into her return mom underwent a spiritual revival that exceeded all of the very emotionally rich and fulfilling, enlightening experiences she previously held dear. Yet, the power of a moment is relative to a particular situation. In that vein, all the spirit-filled friends mom communed with prior to returning home unwittingly played a hand in grooming her for the next level of her growth that was presently manifesting itself. Mom believed the pattern of her life began unfolding when she was but a child, sitting at the feet of one grandmother, being versed in folklore and spiritual teachings; going to country revivals with the other; and following both grandpas around as they talked about moon signs, and planted and harvested their gardens. These experiences gave her an edge in being able to converse with the more folkloric traditions of her southern culture. While she pursued and achieved education through the Doctorate level, traveling this country and the world, meeting the famous and not-so-famous, and achieving in her field, she never lost the part of herself that was so richly spawned during her childhood years. She could sit through a seven-course meal, correctly using every utensil, conversing with the effete, and at the drop of a hat, without batting an eye, kick off her designer shoes and eat collard greens and cornbread with her fingers under the humblest conditions. This was the same mom who, when doing research for her dissertation, saw something taking place in black fundamentalist churches that put her in awe, raised her curiosity, and thrust her on a spiritual quest that culminated in her "getting religion" the old-fashioned way. It was this process, getting religion and coming to know women who, while sharing their life-changing experiences with her, taught her to moan before the Lord and tarry at the Mourner's Bench, that she believed played a major role in helping her reach the point in her overall personal development that was sustaining her during this unique circumstance. Only someone who has gone through a similar experience has an inkling of its proportions. There is not a part of you that is not taxed.

Emotionally, mom was losing her mom and physically she was losing her mom. If she thought about it really hard, she could say it had been years since she had a relationship with grandma as a confidante. She was consumed by a feeling of emptiness when grandma was first diagnosed but to be in the midst of a situation where you see changes firsthand on a day-to-day basis takes your personal feelings to a higher level of intensity.

Mom's losses were compounded by the deaths of two individuals who were more than just friends. One was a playmate of her early childhood years, who was also a cousin; the other was a spiritual sister and confidante of her mature years. In the midst of these losses, and at the center of mom's being was God, the force that truly kept her together. She talked to Him and wrote letters in which she poured out her heart to Him of her losses, her feelings of despair, her frustrations, needs – everything. And when she looks back on those letters and the journal she kept, she has proof that God heard her and met her needs. In situations such as hers, she says only Holy Ghost power will work. She learned to trust Him in every circumstance because only He knows what is best. She could not see the whole picture so she did not truly know what to ask God for. She had to put faith to work and let Him meet the need. It was during the seventh year of mom's return that God did just that with the Hallelujah Lady, Miss Sunshine, and Baby Sis.

Who was giving mom pep talks midst this very demanding situation? She was sustained by her deep faith in the power of God. Each time something occurred to make everything work together, she saw it as God's hand in the matter. This was how she got her pep. Then there were her times in the yard. She dug, transplanted, uprooted, put out fertilizer, and mowed the lawn; for a while, she did it all. Placing her hands on the earth put her in tune with the universe, and like clockwork, she repeated the process to keep her soul at peace and her mind and spirit strengthened.

There had been a constant flow of aides in the home now. During mom's last year working three states away, I came to grandma's to help out. Moving into their basement apartment, I secured a job, and became mom's informant. Mom never asked me to do this. I decided to, wanted to, and while my presence filled a need, I soon realized neither my experience nor maturity were equal to the tremendous task that engulfed me. In some ways, I may have heightened mom's stress level, but at least, someone was there seeing firsthand what was taking place.

By the time mom returned home, our need for sitters exceeded that for aides. Sitters were there to keep grandpa and grandma from being alone, heat dinner, and serve them when mom worked late. The distinction of "sitter", the pay offered, and the lack of medical skill required led to an interesting mix of individuals. It was obvious grandpa was having great difficulty adjusting to their presence. He measured the overall demeanor and efficiency of these sitters against the palette of qualities he admired in his friends. Almost every day he had to be reminded of the reality of our needs and the ensuing flexibility we would have to exercise in having this need met. As trying as the immediate presence of all these individuals may have been, their presence in the home brought "color" to the day-to-day routine aspects of caring for physically challenged parents.

An important routine for the weekend was going to church on Sunday. For the first two years of mom's return home everybody got up on Sunday morning and, miraculously, we went to church, arriving on time, wheelchair and all.

As grandma's condition deteriorated, grandpa went and mom stayed home with grandma. However, as much as mom tried, she could not make up for the lack of time spent fellowshipping with the Saints. All along she thought she was doing fine and she was if you looked at how she was able to keep appointments, make schedules, and, keep the home stocked with groceries and medical supplies. It was the part you could not see, the inner man, that was in sore need of revival. Her change came after she attended an in-home prayer meeting led by the evangelist daughter of a friend with whom she worked. She left the meeting with renewed spiritual hunger and strength and vowed to visit "the little white church" up the street. By this time, she and grandpa had begun alternating their Sunday church time and she was feeling better spiritually because she had every other Sunday to look forward to.

As for grandma, she was well into the world she was creating for herself. Her legs were becoming stiff and straightening them out to stand her up was almost impossible. She was no longer able to assist us as we tried to help her remain a physical part of her environment but true to the spirit of grandma we were accustomed to from the past, she discovered a way to keep herself involved. With her legs stiffly straightened, she rhythmically tapped her heels on the floor, as if she were part of an ensemble. She kept a consistent pattern, "tap, tap, tap, tap," only changing its speed and volume. To this, she added a rustling sound, by quickly moving her hand back and forth on one side of her head. These sounds were enriched by a vocal hum, similar to the kind you hear coming from the amen corner in a fundamentalist church. Grandma had become her own sound box. This was her condition when mom decided to take her to her new-found church.

To an onlooker, these movements and their accompanying audible sounds suggested tension within grandma's spirit, but one thing from her memory of the past that pleased and sometimes quieted her was putting on a hat. Mom was counting on this to make it possible for all of them to sit through church. So, they all buckled up and went to church and it was there that God met the need to the degree of its intensity.

Grandma did sit through the service. Her tapping, rustling, and humming, blended right in with the hand-clapping, foot-stomping, shouting, and outcries of "Praise the Lord" of the congregation. As mom was preparing to return home, the Hallelujah Lady came right up to mom and said, "I will meet you at your house to help get your mom inside because I know where you live." That act of sincere kindness warmed mom's heart and gave evidence to the providence of God because that next week her afternoon sitter moved on to another job and there was no known source of replacement. After church the following Sunday when mom notified the pastor, she was in need of afternoon help, the pastor pointed immediately to the Hallelujah Lady and said, "That's whom you need right there." Mom's assessment of the situation was she was destined to be in that church. Looking back, it was good she had to secure new help because grandma's condition was in a constant state of change. The more involved level of care required a higher level of skill and greater dependability. What the Hallelujah Lady brought into our home was dependability, good work habits, respect for what mom was doing, great personal faith, first-hand relationship with God, and commitment to her beliefs. She possessed a level of basic skill mom had not had in a sitter before. It was not too long after she came that grandma was hospitalized due to dehydration and the Hallelujah Lady was already in place. What a mighty God we serve! There was no question about it, the Hallelujah Lady was a God send and in time the power of her presence for grandma would soon be revealed.

The next change in the level of care arrived through an aide who worked for the agency that provided care in the mornings. Mom called her Ms. Sunshine because she'd come in every morning and greet grandma and grandpa with a kiss on the forehead. She was cheerful by the sound of her voice, her encouraging words, her smiles, and her laughter. She matched the quality of care provided by the Hallelujah Lady. She took charge of every part of grandma's care under her responsibility. No one had done it like this before. She sincerely believed she was there to make a difference in how grandma began and completed her day. She did not simply bathe and change her; she planned the way she did it and each day's order of care was as if the highest authority in the land was coming to inspect her. Grandma's muscle tone, skin condition, and even her vocal responses improved under Ms. Sunshine's presence and care.

"Look at God", mom often said as she surveyed everything. This was God's situation, but grandpa said, "This is a job few would volunteer for." Yes, he was right but mom said she couldn't help herself. It was as if that magnetic force that drew her to the front of the church when she confessed Jesus at eight years old was propelling her now. That's the way mom explained it spiritually. In the natural, she said she was very much like a military recruit. In both instances, success depended on extraordinary stamina and specialized training under highly qualified leadership which, when compounded together, resulted in your becoming the best you could be. Overall, this was true since mom refused to consider less than success. A few times grandpa had thrown up his hands and moaned, "Let's just go on and do what you are trying to avoid." To which mom replied, "It's too late. I have changed my whole life and made a commitment. How dare you talk of giving up. If you can't give me a positive word, say nothing."

In the case of caregivers, there are books to read for clinical information and medical assessment and support group meetings to attend for sharing the similarity of situations; yet, as far as receiving information that will prepare you for what to expect when you are really in the trenches, so speak, from individuals who have gone through it, mom found it was like pregnancy, menopause, sex after fifty, and other life passages. The experiences are so personal, that few can open up to discuss their intimate aspects of them. Not until you are up to your elbows in diapers, bed sores, a foul breath of decaying teeth, protruding hip bones from wasting muscle tissue, atrophied limbs, dimmed sight, and infantile gibberish, do book and support group meetings become reality. Moreover, you deal with it by responding to each need as it occurs.

This was reality, yet it was not moms alone. Earlier I said grandma's condition affected the entire family. What of Baby Sis, grandma's only surviving sibling?

She lives right next door to grandma and grandpa and looking at her mom saw so many of her family's old ways. Anyway, it would be easier if a ramp connected the two houses because through the years there has been so much in-and-out. Mom's grandma told her stories about when the family lived on "the hill" as the 71st home place is called. There, everyone was in close proximity to the big house of mom's great grandma Emily, who had given each of her children a piece of land after they married. As with all families, there was dissension at times, but, basically, family members walked from house to house sharing food, and during times of crises, they gathered in a central place, usually in someone's yard or on someone's porch, and talked, and talked, and talked.

With grandma having Alzheimer's, Baby Sis is the single immediate relative who remembers or even continues in part those traditions. In her colloquialisms, gait, and gestures, she brings to life some of what mom has shared with me of my great grandpa, the old home place, and its colorful way of life. Baby Sis is not only our strong link to grandma's family traditions, but she also became for mom a cheerleader and leaning post. For mom, this underscored that while Alzheimer's was taking something from us, grandma's condition was giving birth to something truly powerful – a network of one-of-a-kind people realizing purpose that here-to-fore they knew not of.

T hey were not just taking care of someone infirmed, they had become part of a special task force inspired by a commitment to responsibility but sustained by God. It wasn't that mom needed them, God did. How could they not do their very best? For them, God was not a far-removed force out there in the cosmos. They saw Him all around in the difficult situations that arose daily in caring for grandma. They saw Him in mom's faith and in her physical and spiritual strength, and they testified to the uniqueness of this special time in all our lives.

So, there was no sad talk, no depressed moods, and no negative dispositions. Anyway, how could you be sad in grandma's room? White lace roman curtains hung at the windows, highlighted by pink, blue, and white flowered poufs at each corner. Both grandma's hospital bed and grandpa's single bed had matching coverlets. On the walls were two large brightly painted ethnic prints, one of a family reunion picnic and the other of a river baptism. Mom identified with both, though only vicariously with the latter.

As a very young girl, one of the highlights of her Summers was attending revivals at the home church of her maternal grandmother. In that setting, drinking water from the pump and going to the outhouse were not so much inconveniences as they were parts of an exciting adventure that culminated in young people tarrying at the mourner's bench under the prayerful tutelage of the speaker for the event, accompanied by mothers of the church and deaconesses from the Amen corner. The excitement and vitality of these childhood experiences remained stored in her memory to be revived years later during field research for the doctorate. It was in out-of-the-way fundamentalist churches, nestled in rural hamlets that she rekindled images from that idyllic past. Only the players were different as the preacher took center stage, first announcing, then moving on to chant his sermon, replete with stock phrases stored up over the generations; punctuated by responses from the congregation, choir, and Amen corner. As she surveyed it all through the haze of dust that rose from the wooden floor beaten by the rhythmic dancing of shouting saints, all of it took on the eery air of an impressionistic painting. Each time mom entered grandma's room, and began the ritual of physical care, she became part of a reunion of sorts, with ancestors she'd heard of but never met; with those she had known, and with the spirits of all those who had in their own way kept a similar vigil as she, nurturing the essence of a loved one. So then, the prints served as a point of contact with mom and the past, not just her immediate family past but her broad cultural roots and the vestiges of centuries gone by. What they ignited in her memory warmed her heart and strengthened her spirit. Every time she stood by grandma's bed and changed or fed her, talked to her, prayed over her, or helped the minister give her communion, she looked at the print depicting a reunion and she was warmed by thoughts of how the spirit of that scene was alive in her through the energy generated through those who reached out and touched her in kind words, smiles, and thoughtful deeds. In Mom's plan to stimulate grandma, she placed both prints where grandma's eyes could not miss them. In addition to the prints were numerous family photos on the triple dresser. In Mom's mind, the message exuded by all of these visuals massaged the entire room. Above the TV console was a gold leaf framed vintage print of a black angel strumming a washboard as if it were a harp, given to her by her special co-resource worker friend in the school system, and in whom she saw a strong affirming constituent. For mom, that particular print speaks to the presence of angels amongst us. In fact, when her friend gave it to her she said, "I know you have a guardian angel watching over you. When you need to, just look at this and be reminded." Everyone who entered grandma's bedroom spoke of its warmth and beauty. It was definitely not a place to avoid because of the patient's physical condition. There was a wing-back chair and rocker for sitting and a desk where workers sat to write and place notes for mom and the visiting nurse. There was life in that room, love in that room, and a special family history being made in that room.

There was a block of time when the Hallelujah Lady and Ms. Sunshine's time overlapped, so did the Hallelujah Lady's time and that of Baby Sis. When this occurred, it reminded mom of the high energy exchanges between the ladies of bygone days in 71st Township, as they gathered to wash their clothes by the spring, made famous in folklore preserved on the family home place. In grandma's room, you could hear laughter and happy talk and there grandma was in the center of it all. In the middle of diaper and linen changes, and tube feedings, there was vibrancy. Similarly, by the spring where ladies gossiped and washed their clothes underneath the thick canopy of tree limbs, midst wood smoke lilting upward from beneath black iron wash pots, and the rhythmic sounds of clothes being rubbed on washboards in #3 tin tubs; grandma's bedroom, and its accompanying activities, generated their own energy. Even when each lady was there alone there was a special air. You could feel it as you crossed the bedroom threshold. The Hallelujah Lady often said, "You'd have to see it to believe it." There was something special happening in grandma's house.

Those who came to see mom for business reasons even remarked about the warmth they felt in the house. Going no further than the living room or front hall, they responded to the character and feeling of warmth the house exuded.

Lessons

Grandma's condition taught us about many things, especially love. Mom said she not only learned more about who she was as a member of her family, as an individual with traits of both parents, as a relative, as a neighbor, as a member of a community, as a church member, as a Christian believer but as a particle of the universe. Every day in some way she had to see herself as one of these and think it through in order to keep standing, keep moving through a particular given moment. She said grandma took care of her when she was small and was continuing to contribute to her development as an adult. Though grandma didn't plan it, didn't know it, and would stop Alzheimer's if she could, her condition was bringing gifts to mom- gifts in a constant state of being unwrapped. Each day brought a pull of the ribbon, a louder rustle of the wrapping in which the gift was encased, meaning new discoveries and understandings, not like the powerful jolt of being shot from a cannon but more like the consistent, slow, deliberate drip drop of rain on stone. Though the cannon shot gets your attention by its volume, the raindrops are no less an attention getter, the difference is you must listen through the subtlety of their sound.

I feel as if I'm watching a drama unfold. It is not unlike other great dramas occurring on the world's stage. It speaks variously of the stamina, breadth, and depth of the human spirit; integrity of friendship; faith in a spiritual essence that moves on men; and significance of the total life experience. While its backdrop is the altered state of a single human being, the irony is it is giving birth to the self-actualization of many.

When considering my mom, her name is at once a description of something unmovable, unshakeable, and being in a constant state of motion. Is this the timid girl I was told stories of who appeared to lack the competitive edge of those who learned the value of competing and struggling through squabbling with siblings as they rivaled each other? There is no doubt that mom slew all her "Goliaths" and has become herself a symbol of how we are to respond to life's challenges. That is not to lie down and quibble at its frustrations, disappointments, pains, sorrows, and losses; for this is the stuff of which life is made and it is in going through each, one by one, that we master the process that leads to the exhilaration of triumph at prevailing over the complexities of human experience.

Grandma has Alzheimer's but it's o.k. She is still in process; not yet what she shall be. We her family are all there – grandpa, baby sis, great-grandchild, myself, Ever-willing Kind Spirit, mom's dear childhood friend and her family, and the ever-changing palette of aides. There are others who also constitute a nucleus of special people who have bonded through respect for what is taking place in the name of the indomitable will of the human spirit to rise to the occasion.

Grandma is on a journey she cannot describe. She is experiencing it, yet cannot express her perception of it. In watching her day-after-day through weeks, months, and years, we have sensed with greater awe the magnificence of our bodies and how wonderfully and intricately they are made. Rather than a sad time, this is an all-affirming time for what life, with all its transitory moments, can be if we but learn this reality: we have to play the hand we're dealt until it's out. More particularly, we have all learned Alzheimer's is not just a medical moment but family, memories, and friends – a peculiar prism through which all the minute particles of which we are made refract, bursting forth, bombarding others, infusing them with a greater sense of the power of love, the mystery of life, and the strength of faith.

About the Author

D r. Marian Tally Simmons Brown is a retired educator and acknowledged scholar of Afro-American Culture, particularly Music of the Southern Fundamentalist Black Church. She has been a voice of recognizing the seminal power of the Black Church ritual in maintaining Black Culture in Conferences, Workshops, and Seminars throughout her professional career. For twenty years she was a Professor of Fine Arts, at Florida State College, Jacksonville, Florida, participating in its Humanities Abroad Program, accompanying students to select Museums and Architectural sites throughout Europe and also its Group Abroad Program to Sierra Leone, West Africa, sponsored by the United States Department of Education.

In 1992 Dr. Brown was among twenty-six Humanities College faculty selected from Colleges in the Southeastern United States to study

" Texts of the Encounters of Pre-Columbian and Spanish Cultures" in a five-week seminar sponsored by the National Endowment for the Humanities at Johns Hopkins University, Baltimore, Maryland. It was while she was there that her mother's diagnosis of intermediate-stage Alzheimer's was confirmed. At the peak of her career with twenty years of tenure at her place of employment, extensive community and cultural arts activities along with professional commitments Dr. Brown made a conscious decision to return to her birth home and assume the responsibility of primary caregiver for her mother. This was a life-changing decision. An only child, without a committed extended family or an abundance of financial assets, she and her father commit to keeping her mother in the family home for the remainder of her natural life. During the last ten years of her mother's life, Dr. Brown logs the family's struggles as they watch over the mother and witness her transformation.

Told through the voice of the family grandchild this memoir is not only for caregivers and families of Alzheimer's patients but for everyone who cares for someone. Dr. Brown continues to share her experiences in Workshops for Caregivers and those coping with Grief and Women's Empowerment Groups.

www.ingramcontent.com/pod-product-compliance
Lightning Source LLC
Chambersburg PA
CBHW020340130626
46549CB00003B/1232